THE BILL OF RIGHTS
HOW AMENDMENTS ARE ADOPTED

BY RICH SMITH

SERIES CONSULTANT: SCOTT HARR, J.D. CRIMINAL JUSTICE
DEPARTMENT CHAIR, CONCORDIA UNIVERSITY ST. PAUL

VISIT US AT
WWW.ABDOPUBLISHING.COM

Published by ABDO Publishing Company, 8000 West 78th Street, Suite 310, Edina, MN 55439.
Copyright ©2008 by Abdo Consulting Group, Inc. International copyrights reserved in all countries.
No part of this book may be reproduced in any form without written permission from the publisher.
Abdo & Daughters™ is a trademark and logo of ABDO Publishing Company.

Printed in the United States.

Editor: John Hamilton
Graphic Design: John Hamilton
Cover Design: Neil Klinepier
Cover Illustration: Getty Images
Interior Photos and Illustrations: p 1 Constitution & flag, iStockphoto; p 5 Monopoly board, Corbis; p 7 replica of Constitution, iStockphoto; p 9 suffragette marching in parade, Corbis; p 11 President Franklin D. Roosevelt, Corbis; p 13 U.S. Capitol, iStockphoto; p 15 110th Congress sworn in, AP Images; p 16 Al Capone, AP Images; p 17 woman with tire cover, Corbis; p 19 pen & ink on Constitution, iStockphoto; p 20 *Scene at the Signing of the Constitution* by Howard Chandler Christy, National Archives; p 21 Constitution & flag, iStockphoto; p 23 judge with gavel, iStockphoto; p 25 scales and law books, iStockphoto; p 26 child laborer, Corbis; p 27 Scottish Crown Jewels, Corbis, p 29 Constitution at National Archives, Corbis.

Library of Congress Cataloging-in-Publication Data

Smith, Rich, 1954-
  How amendments are adopted / Rich Smith.
    p. cm. -- (The Bill of Rights)
  Includes index.
  ISBN 978-1-59928-922-9
  1. Constitutional amendments--United States--Juvenile literature. I. Title.

  KF4555.Z9S65 2008
  342.7303--dc22

                    2007014532

CONTENTS

INTRODUCTION

America's favorite board game is not checkers, and it's not chess. America's all-time best-selling board game is Monopoly. You know the game: players roll dice to move their pieces around a board, collecting $200 in play money each time they pass "Go," and then losing all their saved-up loot if they land on a property with a hotel owned by a rival player.

It's very likely you've played Monopoly at least once in your life. The company that makes the game has sold approximately 300 million copies of it since 1935. Monopoly is such a big favorite that it has been made in more than 200 official versions. There are versions based on movies, TV shows, and cartoon characters. There are versions based on popular sports. There are versions based on specific cities, states, and countries. There are even versions based on the different branches of America's armed forces. The version most people own is "Number Nine," which first came out in 1935.

Yet no matter which version you're playing, the rules of Monopoly today are pretty much the same as they were in 1935. They also are mostly the same as when Monopoly was invented in 1903, even though it was known then as The Landlord's Game, and was meant not for fun but to teach people about the evils of paying rent.

While the rules are nearly the same today as back then, they are not *exactly* the same. For example, when the Parker Brothers company bought the rights to Monopoly in 1935, it added rules that sped up the game. The biggest change came about 20 years earlier when a rule was introduced to let properties be auctioned. It's a rule that still exists. When your game piece lands on a property nobody yet owns, you can buy it at the printed price. If you decide not to buy it, the banker can hold an auction for it. All of the other players can then bid on that property. So can you. The bidding starts at whatever price the banker decides. The bidding can go up or down from there. But the player who bids the most money is the one who wins that property.

The rule about auctions was added because it helped the game move along faster. What's interesting about it is that most people today ignore the auction rule. Many ignore it because they don't like the hurt feelings it creates. It's very easy to use bidding to trick another player into paying an outrageous sum for property that's not worth very much. People hate being tricked. Especially little kids, who tend to cry when it happens to them.

Many others ignore the auction rule because they like using their own made-up rules. Made-up rules are known as "house rules." Monopoly experts say that house rules are just as valid as the official rules. Some even say that house rules are more valid than official rules because house rules reflect the needs, interests, and desires of the players sitting around that one table.

Why bring all this up in a book about the U.S. Constitution and its Bill of Rights? Because the Constitution and Monopoly have a lot in common. They've both been around a long time. They both are important to millions of people. And they both can be changed as needed while remaining pretty much the same no matter what.

Above: The United States Constitution, like the rules of Monopoly, can change to meet the needs of the people.

It's Alive!

Some experts on the Constitution call it a "living" document. They call it that because they see the Constitution as a sheet of rules and a list of rights that stretches and shrinks to fit the mood of the American people. The Constitution changes to reflect the way citizens think, feel, or believe at any point in time.

It's a fact of nature that people's ideas of right and wrong and good and bad change as years go by. For example, the way the people of the United States thought about ethnicity in 1787 when the Constitution was written is not the same way people think about it today. Back then, people who did not have the light, pinkish skin of those from northern Europe were thought to be inferior, or even less than human. Later, most people came to realize that this was an evil way of thinking. But it was a way of thinking that had found its way into the Constitution.

In Article 1, Section 2, Paragraph 3, the Constitution speaks of two types of Americans: those who are free and those who are slaves. In America at the time of the writing of the Constitution, the only people who were slaves were people from central Africa, or whose ancestors came from there. The Constitution described slaves as counting for only three-fifths of a person. In other words, they were inferior compared to other people.

Most Americans in the late 1700s seemed to be OK with that. But some weren't. They were few at first. Then their numbers grew. They talked to their families and friends and anyone who would listen. Eventually, they convinced the majority of people that the idea of some Americans being less than fully human was wrong.

At this point, the Constitution was clearly out of step with the American people. So they changed the Constitution by adding the Fourteenth Amendment in 1868. This change scratched out Article I, Section 2, Paragraph 3.

Above: A replica of page one of the United States Constitution. As society changes over the years, the Constitution can change to better reflect citizens' attitudes and values.

However, the Fourteenth Amendment had a problem that wasn't fixed until 1920, when the Nineteenth Amendment was added. The problem with the Fourteenth Amendment was that it stated that men were the only people who could vote in America. Most people at the time thought that denying the vote to women was a good thing. But just as with the issue of blacks counting for less than whites, a few people who thought women had every right to vote worked hard at convincing the rest of the nation to change their opinion. By 1920, most people believed women should vote. But women could not vote until the Constitution was changed.

Not everybody agrees that the Constitution is a living document. They agree that it can and should be changed when necessary. But they disagree with the idea that the Constitution should lead. They believe the Constitution should be seen as an anchor and the United States as a giant ship. The purpose of an anchor is to stop a ship that's drifting away from the place where it's parked. Without that anchor, the ship is at the mercy of the ocean's currents. Those currents might then push the ship hundreds or thousands of miles from where it's supposed to be. The ship can become lost, or crash into a reef, where it's smashed to bits and everyone aboard drowns.

The people who dislike the idea of a living Constitution believe that the nation's highest law should not be pulled along by the currents of popular opinion or by the mood swings of the people. For example, on many TV talk shows today everyone is against childhood obesity. Show hosts and their guests are constantly urging the government to pass laws to help overweight kids slim down. But the Constitution says nothing about dieting. Should the Constitution be changed so that it does? The people who see the Constitution as an anchor would say no, because the medical world's knowledge about proper dieting is constantly changing. Any amendment about dieting would probably be outdated as soon as it were added to the Constitution. And the last thing anyone should want is a Constitution all gummed up with amendments written in response to situations that are here today, gone tomorrow.

Above: Mrs. Herbert Carpenter, bearing an American flag, marches in a parade in New York City in 1918 supporting women's suffrage. Women finally gained the right to vote in 1920 after ratification of the Nineteenth Amendment to the U.S. Constitution.

If at First They Don't Succeed, They Can Try, Try Again

AS MANY AS 100 or more requests to add an amendment to the Constitution are brought up during each two-year term of the House of Representatives. Nearly all of those requests are turned down. But the people who make those requests don't usually give up the first time Congress says no. They try, try again.

Since the mid-1980s, the rejected request that has come back from the dead the most is one calling for the repeal of the Twenty-Second Amendment. The Twenty-Second Amendment says the president can't be elected to that office more than twice. It was added to the Constitution in 1951 and was meant to prevent a repeat of what happened with President Franklin D. Roosevelt. He was first elected president in 1932. He ran for re-election in 1936 and won. All presidents before him served two terms and then voluntarily served no more. Roosevelt broke that unwritten rule by running for a third term in 1940, which he also won. Then he was elected again in 1944. He might have gone on to win a fifth term in 1948 had he not died in 1945.

The Twenty-Second Amendment was proposed because many people felt the country would be better off going back to the tradition started by George Washington of having presidents in office for no more than two terms. Most people still feel that way, which is why the request for an amendment to repeal the Twenty-Second Amendment keeps being rejected.

Frequently requested are proposals for amendments to clear up the confusing wording of the Constitution. Common too are those aimed at shortening the leash on government so that it cannot so easily prevent people from fully enjoying certain of their rights.

There are also many requests for proposed amendments intended to fix societal problems. For example, during the 2005-2006 term of Congress, there was a request for an amendment that would give Congress the power to regulate how much money

Above: President Franklin D. Roosevelt delivers a radio address to the nation. Roosevelt won four consecutive presidential elections in the 1930s and 1940s. The Twenty-Second Amendment was ratified in 1951 because most people felt the country would be better off if a president only served for two terms.

that a politician could spend out of his or her own pocket when running for office. In the term before that, there was a request for an amendment that would make sure the word "God" is never removed from the Pledge of Allegiance or from the national motto on American coins.

Make a Proposal

Whether you compare the Constitution to a living document or to an anchor, the fact remains that it can be changed. The first time the Constitution was changed was in 1791 with the addition of the 10 amendments making up the Bill of Rights. It was changed 17 more times after that. The most recent change was in 1992.

However, changing the Constitution is not easy. The Framers of the Constitution made sure of that. They did not want future generations playing silly games with the Constitution. They did not want future Americans turning the Constitution into something completely different from what it was in the beginning. They wanted it to last. They made changing it hard in order to discourage people from even trying, but they did not make it so hard that changing the Constitution would be impossible.

The Constitution can be changed by two formal methods and one informal way. The two formal methods are described in the Constitution itself. They are found in Article V.

The first formal way the Constitution can be changed is by having the Senate and House of Representatives propose an amendment. Only 33 times in the nation's history has this happened, even though Congress receives as many as 50 or more requests to make such proposals each and every year.

A proposed amendment begins its journey to join the Constitution with a joint resolution from the House and Senate. Two-thirds of the House members who are present and two-thirds of the senators who are present must vote "yes" on the joint resolution in order for an amendment to be considered proposed. And there must be enough representatives and senators present to count for what is known as a *quorum*. A quorum is the smallest number of members needed in order to officially conduct House or Senate business.

Above: The United States Capitol building in Washington, D.C., where the Senate and the House of Representatives meet to create laws, including proposed amendments to the Constitution.

Because the amendment is proposed through a joint resolution, there is no need to send it to the president for signing, which is required of regular bills passed by Congress. Since the president doesn't sign the resolution, he has no authority to veto it if he thinks it's a bad proposal.

A joint resolution starts out by saying something like this: *"Proposing an amendment to the Constitution of the United States to repeal the Twenty-Fifth Amendment to that Constitution. Resolved by the Senate and House of Representatives of the United States of America in Congress assembled (two-thirds of each House concurring therein), That the following article is proposed as an amendment to the Constitution of the United States...."* (That, by the way, was from an actual joint resolution.) The introductory words of the joint resolution are then followed by the text of the proposed amendment itself.

Next, the proposed amendment contained in that joint resolution is sent to all of the states for their approval. Three-fourths of all the states must approve the proposed amendment for it to become part of the Constitution. Giving such approval is called *ratification*. Since America currently has 50 states, a proposed amendment is considered ratified if 38 states vote in favor of it.

It's up to each state to decide how it wants to handle the job of ratifying a proposed constitutional amendment. The usual way is to have the proposal debated and then voted on by the legislature, just as would be done with any other state law under consideration. The less common way is to hold a ratifying convention. Only one time did Congress require the states to ratify an amendment with the convention method. That was for the Twenty-First Amendment, which made drinking alcohol legal in America once more in 1933.

A ratifying convention is a big meeting attended by people from every part of the state. The people then debate and vote on the proposed amendment. People who attend this convention are called *delegates*. They can be chosen by the state legislature, by the governor, or by the voting public in a special election.

Above: Members of the 110th Congress are sworn in at the U.S. Capitol in Washington, D.C., January 4, 2007. Two-thirds of members present in both the Senate and the House of Representatives must vote "yes" on a joint resolution for a constitutional amendment before it can be sent to the states for ratification.

Once a state ratifies an amendment, there are no take-backs. It can't vote for an amendment and then later change its mind. On the other hand, a state *can* change its mind about an amendment it turned down. If it chooses, a state can reschedule a vote on the rejected amendment and then ratify it.

It used to be that states could take all the time they wanted to think about an amendment before voting on it. For example, the states waited about 200 years before finally ratifying the Twenty-Seventh Amendment. That one was first proposed in 1789, and was actually supposed to be part of the Bill of Rights. Another amendment that was meant to be included in the Bill of Rights—the original First Amendment—*still* hasn't been ratified to this day.

Some people find it wonderful that the states can even now be debating about proposed amendments from way back in time. But others think it is tragic. That's why Congress got in the habit after a while of putting time limits on amendments it sent out to the states. Congress started doing this beginning with the Eighteenth Amendment, which it proposed in 1917. The Eighteenth Amendment outlawed the buying and selling of alcoholic beverages. The amendment is often blamed for bringing to power gangsters like Al Capone, who made huge fortunes and became very powerful by supplying illegal whiskey and other types of liquor to a thirsty nation.

Left: A police mugshot of Al Capone, taken while the notorious gangster was in custody in Philadelphia, Pennsylvania, May 18, 1929. Capone was one of several gangsters who became rich and powerful during Prohibition. The Eighteenth Amendment, which prohibited the manufacture and sale of alcoholic beverages, is often blamed in part for the rise of organized crime in the United States. Gangsters such as Capone made their fortunes partly by smuggling and selling illegal liquor.

Above: In 1930, a woman in Chicago, Illinois, puts a tire cover on her car that demands the repeal of the Eighteenth Amendment, which outlawed the sale of alcoholic drinks. Ratified in 1919, the Eighteenth Amendment is the only constitutional amendment that was later repealed (by the Twenty-First Amendment, which was ratified in 1933).

Never Before Been Done

The second of the two formal ways of changing the United States Constitution is by a method never before done. It is known as a constitutional convention. Article V of the Constitution says that a constitutional convention is to be held if at least two-thirds of the state legislatures ask for one. That means at least 34 out of 50 states must make the request, and the request must be made to Congress.

Congress so far has received more than 500 requests for a constitutional convention. Every state in the union has applied at least once. The holder of the record for asking the most number of times is South Dakota, with 27 requests since winning statehood in 1889. The last time any state requested a constitutional convention was in 1982. The first state to ask for one was Virginia, in 1789, just a year after the Constitution took effect.

Congress requires states to specify why they want a constitutional convention when asking for one. The reason most often given is so that states can propose an amendment to make the mapping of congressional districts more fair. Another reason, one that scares Congress and many other people, is the desire to rewrite the entire Constitution from top to bottom.

States have come close on three occasions to getting a constitutional convention. Twice their requests fell just two states short of the minimum needed. The other time, it was only one state short.

Facing page: A reenactor puts his name on a replica of the United States Constitution using a quill and ink. Some people worry that a state-proposed constitutional convention might result in a totally new form of government. So far, this method of changing the Constitution has never occurred.

Above: Scene at the Signing of the Constitution by artist Howard Chandler Christy.

If it ever happens that a constitutional convention is convened, the delegates who attend will find they are able to draft a proposed amendment. They will be able to debate it. They will be able to make changes to the draft and improve it to everyone's liking. They will be able to vote on whether or not to send it to the state legislatures for ratification. What the delegates will not be able to do is ratify the amendment themselves. As with an amendment proposed by Congress, an amendment put together at a convention must win the approval of three-fourths of all the states in the Union in order to become part of the Constitution.

However, because there has not been a constitutional convention since 1787, no rules exist to tell how the delegates to a constitutional convention today would be picked. And no rules exist to tell how the convention itself would be conducted. More than likely, those rules would have to be made up by Congress and then looked at very closely by the courts to make sure they are fair.

The most important question Congress and the courts would have to answer in making up convention rules deals with the work of the delegates. Delegates would need to know whether they can write an amendment as requested by the states or whether they can create additional amendments that no one has even asked for. Or, could they go further still and give the Constitution and its Bill of Rights a complete makeover? What about throwing the Constitution in the trash can and starting over from scratch with an all-new set of rules for how the government is to be organized and operated? Would that be allowed?

How far the delegates can go is what worries many people the most about a constitutional convention. The men who wrote the Constitution in 1787 were deep thinkers and very careful about what they were doing. The fear is that the delegates to a modern constitutional convention might not be anywhere near as thoughtful or careful. The changes they come up with might make the Constitution much worse instead of better.

In the years following ratification of the Constitution, states turned in 22 applications to ask for a constitutional convention so that they could change the whole document. The last time a state made such a request was 1929.

Below: A replica of the Constitution on top of a flag of the United States.

CHANGES FROM THE BENCH

Having Congress propose amendments and having the states do it through a convention are the two formal ways of changing the Constitution. The third way of doing it is much less complicated, and is very common. It's the informal method known as *judicial review,* which is sort of like the "house rules" in the game of Monopoly.

Part of the job of the courts all across the nation is to consider whether the laws passed by Congress and by the state legislatures are constitutional. A law that is constitutional is one that follows the rules of the Constitution and the Bill of Rights, or any of the other amendments. A law that is not constitutional gets thrown out. This is what judicial review is all about.

Judges almost always give detailed explanations of how and why they make their decisions in lawsuits. Sometimes, those explanations are so good and convincing that they change people's understanding of what the Constitution says and means. The best example of this is the 1803 case of *Marbury v. Madison.* Until the Supreme Court decided this case, most people believed the Constitution gave the courts no power of judicial review. They believed that because there was nothing in the Constitution specifically about judicial review. But the Supreme Court said it didn't matter that the Constitution was silent on this issue. A person only needs to use a little logic to see that the Constitution not only allows judicial review, it requires it, according to the High Court. The explanation was that judges lacking the power of judicial review would be unable to perform the job everyone expected of them. When people heard this explanation, they usually found themselves agreeing with the Supreme Court. And by agreeing, the people were in effect saying they accepted this informal change to the Constitution.

Above: A common informal method of changing the Constitution is judicial review, which involves judges deciding whether laws are constitutional and then writing detailed explanations of how they made their decisions. Sometimes these decisions are so insightful that they change people's understanding of the Constitution.

Judges use several different ways of thinking to guide them as they exercise their power of judicial review. The first way of thinking involves a philosophy called *developmentalism*. Judges who embrace developmentalism are not too concerned about what the Framers of the Constitution meant or intended when the document was first put together more than 200 years ago. Instead, they are mainly concerned with understanding how the rules spelled out by the Constitution can or should apply in the United States of today. Developmentalists take into consideration earlier decisions from other courts. But they balance those against current events, the workings of modern society, and the widely held beliefs, values, and ideals of American culture.

Another way of thinking that judges use involves a philosophy known as *doctrinalism*. Doctrinalists believe the path to the future is made clear by things that have occurred in the past. They look at earlier decisions of other courts and decide which ones made sense and which ones didn't in light of current circumstances. Then they build on those earlier decisions in arriving at decisions of their own.

A third philosophy is *originalism*. This is where judges decide the constitutionality of a law by first trying to understand what the men who wrote the Constitution intended with the words they used. Originalists believe that the more things change in this world, the more they stay the same. To their thinking, the things people worried about and had to deal with in the late 1700s are not really all that different from the things people worry about and deal with today. Sure, there was no Internet at the birth of the United States. But there were printing presses. And isn't the Internet very similar to an electronic version of a printing press? Therefore, an originalist judge would reason, the constitutional issues surrounding the sharing of ideas and opinions back then are much the same as they are today. As a result, originalists pay close attention to how the wise leaders at the country's founding thought about things.

Above: Judges must weigh many factors when deciding whether a law is constitutional or not. Developmentalism, doctrinalism, and originalism are different ways of interpreting the role of the Constitution and how it relates to laws today.

PROPOSED AMENDMENTS STILL FLOATING AROUND

THE BILL OF RIGHTS includes the first 10 amendments to the United States Constitution. Since the adoption of the Bill of Rights in 1791, the Constitution has been amended 17 additional times. The last amendment was adopted in 1992, nearly 200 years after it was offered to the states for ratification. It was originally included in the package of proposed amendments making up the Bill of Rights.

There are four other proposed amendments from long ago still floating around out there. If enough states ratify them, these four could yet become part of the Constitution. One of them was also supposed to be in the Bill of Rights.

The youngest of the four was proposed in 1924. It was an amendment to give Congress the authority to prevent children from doing tough jobs meant for adult men and women. In those days, it was not unusual for kids under the age of 12 to

Below: Addie Laird, a 10-year-old spinner in a cotton mill in Vermont in 1910.

be employed in factories or coal mines. The jobs given to children were often the dirtiest and most tiring. Until the early part of the 20th century, child labor was an accepted fact of life. Then people's attitudes about it changed. But Congress had no power under the Constitution to do anything about child labor. So the Constitution had to be changed. However, the country lost interest in the proposed child labor amendment when the Supreme Court ruled that Congress actually did have power under the Constitution to take action, even though there was nothing specific in the document about child labor. And so the problem of child labor was solved without the need for a constitutional amendment.

One of the oldest of the four proposed amendments still up for ratification deals with titles of nobility. This proposal was sent to the states in 1810. It said that any American citizen who became a duke, a knight, or some other kind of royal titleholder in another country like Great Britain, would lose his or her American citizenship. That's how much America wanted to move away from its colonial past and become a new kind of nation, where everybody is supposed to be equal. In countries where there is royalty, or a dictatorship, people are usually very unequal. The people who are royal are given the best of everything, while the people who are not royal get whatever's left over.

The very oldest of the four proposals started out as the original First Amendment in the Bill of Rights. The states weren't too thrilled with this one because its purpose was to limit the number of representatives that a state could send to Congress. The way things were set up by the Constitution in Article I, Section 2, Clause 3, each state could send to Congress one representative for every 30,000 people living within its boundaries. The more people living in a state, the more representatives it could send. A cap on the number of representatives meant that a state trying to give itself a bigger voice in government could only sound so loud no matter how many residents it attracted. That's why the states have never been too eager to ratify this amendment.

Above: The Scottish Crown Jewels are carried into the Scottish Parliament building in Edinburgh, Scotland. A proposed amendment to the U.S. Constitution would require anyone who gained a foreign title of nobility to lose his or her American citizenship.

CONCLUSION

In 2006, Americans cast more than three million votes to decide how the game of Monopoly should be changed to make it more interesting, more fun, and more relevant to the people who love playing it.

The first thing the voters changed was the street names. They wanted Boardwalk changed to Times Square, and they wanted Park Place to become Fenway Park. Next, they increased the rents. They wanted players who land on Times Square to pay $20 million if that space has a hotel. Also, they turned the four railroad spaces into airports. Further, voters revised the reasons players must "go directly to jail" to include offenses such as identity theft and insider trading. What's more, Community Chest cards were updated so that players no longer would win $10 in a beauty contest, but instead would receive $100,000 for appearing in a reality TV show.

As the company that makes Monopoly explained, the changes were meant to create a "game play experience that more closely matches today's America." Many feel that the Constitution should also more closely match today's America. Others feel it already does, and has since the day it was first written. But the simple fact that people could believe those two very different things about the Constitution and both be right about it at the same time shows how truly amazing the Constitution is. As a rules sheet, it contains instructions for how the very serious game of government is to be played. Yet, if people feel the instructions no longer work for them, they are free to change them. It takes time and hard work to change the Constitution. However, that's exactly what the Constitution was designed to do: change. Even while it stays the same.

Above: A security guard stands alongside the United States Constitution inside the Rotunda for the Charters of Freedom, at the National Archives in Washington, D.C.

GLOSSARY

AMENDMENT

When it was created, the Constitution wasn't perfect. The Founding Fathers wisely added a special section. It allowed the Constitution to be changed by future generations. This makes the Constitution flexible. It is able to bend to the will of the people it governs. Changes to the Constitution are called amendments. The first 10 amendments are called the Bill of Rights. An amendment must be approved by two-thirds of both houses of Congress. Once that happens, the amendment must be approved by three-fourths of the states. Then it becomes law. This is a very difficult thing to do. The Framers of the Constitution didn't want it changed unless there was a good reason. There have been over 9,000 amendments proposed. Only 27 of them have been ratified, or made into law. Some amendments changed the way our government works. The Twelfth Amendment changed the way we elect our president. The Twenty-Second Amendment limits a president to two terms in office. Constitutional amendments have also increased the freedoms of our citizens. The Thirteenth Amendment finally got rid of slavery. And the Nineteenth Amendment gave women the right to vote.

DICTATORSHIP

A country with a single leader who rules with total power. Citizens of a dictatorship have little or no say in how their country is run. Dictators usually gain their position, and keep their powers, through the use of military force. The Constitution was written to avoid dictatorships. It splits government into three distinct parts: the presidency, Congress, and the Supreme Court. This separation of power keeps any one individual from becoming a dictator.

FOUNDING FATHERS

The men who participated in the Constitutional Convention in 1787, especially the ones who signed the Constitution. Some of the Founding Fathers included George Washington, Benjamin Franklin, John Rutledge, Gouverneur Morris, Alexander Hamilton, and James Madison.

High Court

Another name for the United States Supreme Court.

Lawsuit

A legal way to settle a dispute in which both sides argue their case in front of a judge or jury in a court of law. The person who has been wronged is called the plaintiff. The person being sued is called the defendant. Plaintiffs and defendants can be individuals, or they can be businesses or government entities, such as corporations or towns. People can even sue the United States, which is how many cases are filed involving the Constitution and violation of rights.

Prohibition

A period of time in the United States, from 1920 to 1933, when the selling, manufacturing, or transporting of alcohol for beverages was prohibited.

Ratification

The process of making a proposed law or treaty officially valid. Constitutional amendments are ratified when they are approved by two-thirds of both houses of Congress, and by three-fourths of the states.

Suffrage

The right to vote in a political election. The Nineteenth Amendment, ratified in 1920, gave women suffrage.

Supreme Court

The United States Supreme Court is the highest court in the country. There are nine judges on the Supreme Court. They make sure local, state, and federal governments are following the rules spelled out in the United States Constitution. Our understanding of the Constitution evolves over time. It is up to the Supreme Court to decide how the Constitution is applied to today's society. When the Supreme Court rules on a case, other courts in the country must follow the decision in similar situations. In this way, the laws of the Constitution are applied equally to all Americans.

INDEX